The Perils of Pixie

By Kimberly M. Kimbler

Illustrated by Becky Hochhalter

Archway Publishing, Bloomington, Indiana

Archway Publishing books may be ordered through booksellers or by contacting:

Archway Publishing
1663 Liberty Drive
Bloomington, IN 47403
www.archwaypublishing.com
844-669-3957

Interior Image Credit: Becky Hochhalter

Scripture taken from the King James Version of the Bible.

ISBN: 978-1-6657-0216-4 (sc)
ISBN: 978-1-6657-0217-1 (hc)
ISBN: 978-1-6657-0215-7 (e)

Print information available on the last page.

Archway Publishing rev. date: 02/12/2021

This book is dedicated to the joys in my life,
the memory of my Mother and Father, my daughter and sons
and my loving husband.

**Being rich in the love of
all my family, friends and pets
is God's greatest gift.**

This interactive book is a wonderful way to look up Bible verses
with your children. Some of my most memorable and favorite
Bible verses are ones learned at a younger age.

Be brave... Psalms 27:14

With ice on my paws
and snow on my back,
wish I could find a spot
for a warm winter snack.

I asked a stray cat
which way should I go,
he said, "Just do your best
and get out of the snow."

Guidance . . . Psalms 119:105

Finding direction... Psalms 32:8

If I knew where I was
if I had been where I came,
I could find my way back,
just as if I weren't lame.

I limped to the left
and then to the right,
I felt something lift me
clean out of sight.

Finding hope. . . Psalms 71:14

Needing nourishment. . . Genesis 50:21

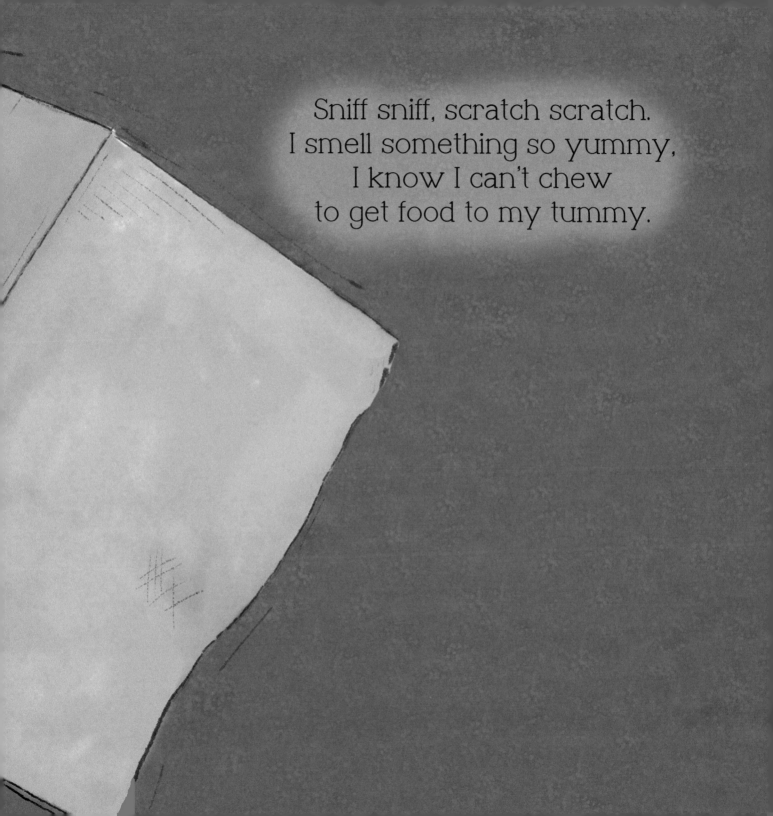

Sniff sniff, scratch scratch.
I smell something so yummy,
I know I can't chew
to get food to my tummy.

She scooped me up.
I could tell I'd be safe,
when others said, "No, I can't."
she said, "I can't wait."

Feeling safe . . . Psalms 119:117

I feel I am moving
to where I don't know,
even though I feel warmth
okay... here we go.

Keep moving forward... Proverbs 3:6

Be strong . . . Psalms 27:14

The big roof is so green
the building so bright.
I hope they will help me
so I can take bites.

I smell another cat
and there are dogs here too,
more people with smiles
and they're glad to see you.

Be glad... Psalms 16:9

Time of healing . . . Psalms 147:3

Charlie

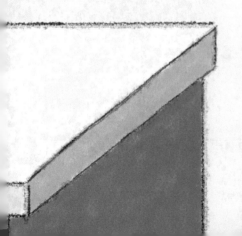

She looked in my ears
and opened my mouth,
don't poke me, don't stick me.
She even looked up my snout.

The surgery is done,
and nothing to fear,
all I remember is,
"You take care my dear!"

Always be happy... 1 Thessalonians 5:16

Heal me . . . Jeremiah 17:14

She said, "Your puppy is ready,
but will need some special care."
She asked for my name,
then I heard the trumpets blare.

My owner said, "PIXIE",
I bounced up with joy.
I scampered and scurried,
my life can now be enjoyed!

All of a sudden,
I smell food and feel fluff,
I'm beginning each day
with a wag, twirl, and a RUFF!

Provide safe shelter... Isaiah 32:18

Remember each night,
when you lay down your head,
ask for faith, strength and courage,
with your prayers being said.

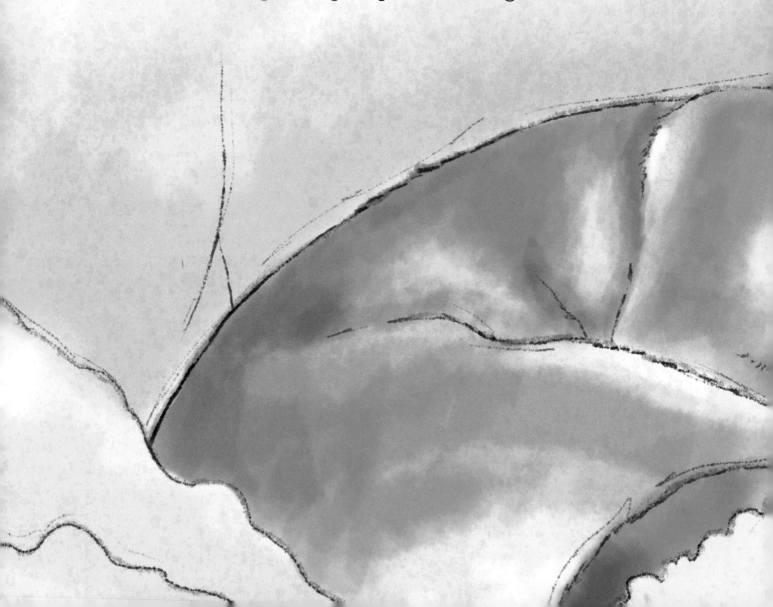

peaceful sleep... Proverb 3:24

Pixie's Story

This story was inspired by true events beginning with the cold frigid night air. This small orphaned chihuahua's journey begins with cars speeding by and a fierce tiger cat chasing her down a cold and icy alley. The sun was just ready to peer over the tops of the cars as the humans sped by to get to their favorite breakfast spot, Cackleberries. All this chihuahua could think about was a nice warm meal and then all of a sudden she could smell the aroma of bacon from a nearby restaurant. This puppy knew the grumbling in her tummy could not go on much longer.

Without a leash, collar or name tag, this chihuahua felt so lost and just wanted a place to stay warm. The shivering puppy looked to the tiger cat for answers on which way to go. The cat was no help and it seemed like the lost and shivering puppy had been running loose for a long time. You could see her rib bones with her big brown eyes and loose teeth.

Not every pet may have a perfect life and we may not always know where they have strayed from, especially since dogs cannot speak to us. Although they can speak through emotions. They give us their emotions through their eyes, when they wag their tail or when they sulk like they are sad. However, just think what dogs could tell you if they could talk? As we think about what this little shivering puppy has been through, she longs for a sense of security; a puppy's natural instinct is always survival.

Thus, off we went to a place I knew would give this chihuahua hope to live. Where this tattered soul could improve and get healthier without a moment to waste. I felt the best place to restore her back to health was Heritage Animal Hospital. They went to work on her immediately. She was a possible 2.5 pounds and very listless. All her teeth were loose and poking to the front of her mouth. The Veterinarians, Dr. Pat and Dr. Jessica, felt she was possibly about 7 years old and would need a couple surgeries.

Caring for one another and all God's creations is how we are taught from a very young age. Even though I thought this chihuahua was only going to stay temporarily, since we searched for her home, it ended up that her attachment to me was a bond you sometimes feel instantly. After her veterinarian care, she started to perk right up and feel right at home in her fluffy warm bed each night.

Pet adoption has grown to help decrease dogs and cats being euthanized in local shelters. You can find wonderful pets of all breeds and sizes through rescue. It may not be that the pet was unwanted, it may be the owner may have passed away or someone was unable to give care to that pet.

The moral to this story; a pet may not always be someone you select, He or She may select you. Pixie had my heart from the very start.

Fun objects to hunt throughout this book:

Purple Bicycle = BS
Artist Brush = BH
Yellow Daisy = CC
Brown Owl = CS
Terrier "Bodie" = ES
Red Tricycle = JC
Blue Bird = KK
Pink Ribbon = KR
Two Rings = LK
Red Ball = SM

About the Author

Kimberly M. Kimbler is a nursing student advisor at Indiana State University. For the past thirty years, she has been a tireless volunteer who has assisted organizations with fulfilling missions of helping children with basic needs and saving the environment. She resides in Terre Haute, Indiana. This is her first book.

About the Illustrator

Becky Hochhalter is a self-taught artist who has been creating art since childhood. For over thirty years, she has worked within a diverse range of mediums including murals, traditional commissioned paintings and drawings, digital paintings and illustrations, photography, and sculpture. Becky resides in Terre Haute, Indiana.

Printed in the United States
by Baker & Taylor Publisher Services